W9-CGY-036

The Nature and Science of SEEDS

Jane Burton and Kim Taylor

Gareth Stevens Publishing
MILWAUKEE

For a free color catalog describing Gareth Stevens Publishing's list of high-quality books and multimedia programs, call 1-800-542-2595 (USA) or 1-800-461-9120 (Canada). Gareth Stevens Publishing's Fax: (414) 225-0377.

Library of Congress Cataloging-in-Publication Data

Burton, Jane.
The nature and science of seeds / by Jane Burton and Kim Taylor.
p. cm. — (Exploring the science of nature)
Includes bibliographical references and index.
Summary: Describes the nature, dispersal,
growth, and uses of seeds.
ISBN 0-8368-2184-X (lib. bdg.)
1. Seeds—Juvenile literature. 2. Seeds—Dispersal—
Juvenile literature. 3. Germination—Juvenile literature.
[1. Seeds.] I. Taylor, Kim. II. Title.
III. Series: Burton, Jane. Exploring the science of nature.
QK661.B87 1999
581.4'67—dc21 98-34023

First published in North America in 1999 by
Gareth Stevens Publishing
1555 North RiverCenter Drive, Suite 201
Milwaukee, Wisconsin 53212 USA

Printed in the United States of America

1 2 3 4 5 6 7 8 9 03 02 01 00 99

14,95

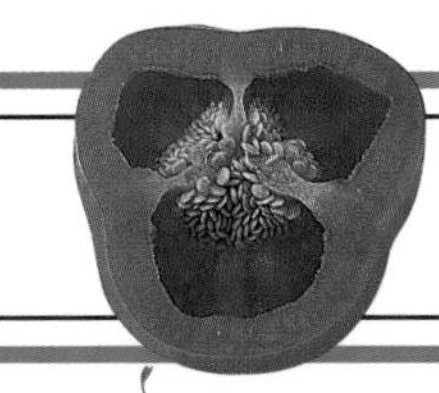

Contents

Words that appear in the glossary are printed in **boldface** type the first time they occur in the text.

Plants Make Seeds

Top: A young oak tree bursts from a rounded, smooth acorn.

A seed is something special. It can look plain and uninteresting on the outside. On the inside, however, it has all the magical elements needed to start a new plant.

Seeds can blow in the wind or get kicked around in the dust, sometimes for years. Then, when conditions allow, they suddenly begin to grow. Some seeds are no bigger than grains of sand, yet they grow into huge trees!

Plants make seeds so that new plants will grow. Each seed contains a **food store**. Another part of the seed called the **embryo** contains information that is needed for the seed to grow. The embryo is joined to the food store. It may be composed of just a few **cells**, or it may look like a miniature plant. A **seed coat** surrounds each seed.

Seeds form in the flowers of plants when **pollen** grains (male cells) join with **ova** (female cells). Each seed contains information from both its parents. When a plant grows, it may look partly like one parent and partly like the other.

Above: A split peanut reveals the embryo, which is normally hidden between the two halves of the food store.

Below: Every enormous redwood tree grows from a tiny seed.

Opposite: Giant redwoods (or sequoias) are some of the biggest living things on Earth. They can reach 330 feet (100 meters) into the sky.

Seeds Make Plants

Top: A cactus produces small black seeds that remain on the plant for a long time.

In order for a seed to grow into a new plant, it must meet certain conditions. Seeds will not **germinate** without water. A tiny hole, called a **micropyle**, in the seed coat allows water inside. As water soaks in, the seed starts to swell.

Water is just one requirement for a germinating seed; **oxygen** is another. The seed needs to breathe, so it must take in oxygen. Oxygen breaks down the food store, releasing energy for growth. Seeds buried too deep in the ground may not germinate because there is not enough oxygen deep in the soil.

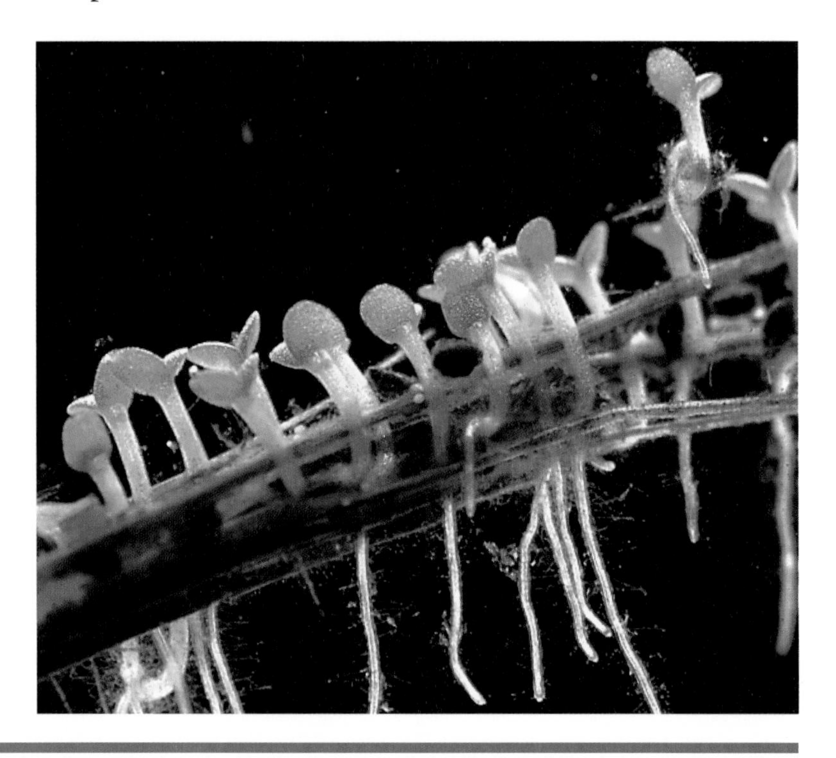

Right: A seed **pod** of rosebay willowherb has fallen into a pond, and all the seeds in it have germinated. The white **roots** grow downward, and the green **shoots** grow upward.

Left: Seeds beneath an acacia tree stayed there many months until heavy rains caused them to germinate.

Seeds also need warmth to germinate. Many seeds will not germinate until the temperature is at least 59° **Fahrenheit** (15° **Centigrade**).

A germinating seed eventually bursts its seed coat and emerges as a white spike. This is the first root. The root "knows" which way is up and which way is down. It always bends so that it grows downward.

The part of the root that is sensitive enough to know exactly which way to grow is at the tip. If the tip were to be somehow cut off, the root would grow in any direction.

Above: The seed coat of a scarlet runner bean splits as the root emerges. The root turns and begins to grow downward.

The shoot of the bean pulls itself out from between the two halves of the food store and starts to grow upward.

A pair of leaves opens. Leaf-like structures called **cotyledons** in the seed coat serve as a source of food for the bean plant.

The young bean plant now has two leaves and a mass of roots. A shoot reaches for the sky.

It makes sense for a root emerging from a seed to grow downward. The root needs to be in the ground to take in moisture and **minerals** for the growing plant. It also makes sense for a shoot to grow upward, but shoots are not as sensitive to direction as roots. They are, however, sensitive to light. As an example, shoots growing from seeds placed in a dark box with a small hole in the top or side will aim for the hole. They reach for the light and eventually pop through the hole.

The food store in a seed is made of **starch, protein**, and oil. Sometimes, the food store is contained in a special part of the seed called the **endosperm**. Some seeds have no endosperm. Then, the food is stored in the embryo. The food stores of peas and beans are in the first pair of leaves. When the pea or bean seedling grows, its first leaves shrivel as the food in them is used up.

When most seeds germinate and start to grow, they produce one or a pair of leaf-like structures called cotyledons. These structures are often a different shape from the leaves that are produced later. Cotyledons of peas and beans become the food stores for these plants.

Above: The two folded cotyledons of a seedling beech tree push up through fallen leaves.

Next, the cotyledons spread out to catch the light.

Eventually, a shoot appears from between the cotyledons.

Below: A pair of beech leaves opens above the cotyledons.

Flowering plants are divided into two groups — according to whether they have one or two cotyledons.

Grasses and lilies have only one cotyledon and are grouped together as **monocotyledons**. Peas, beans, and most other flowering plants have two cotyledons. Structures with two cotyledons are known as **dicotyledons**.

Sleeping Seeds

Top: Beech seeds drop to the ground when they become ripe in autumn. They lie there in rain and snow but do not germinate until spring.

Seeds that have plenty of oxygen, warmth, and water still do not always germinate. It is as if the seeds are asleep and need something to wake them. Some seeds may stay in the ground for years without germinating because their seed coats are tough and waterproof. Even though these seeds are surrounded by damp soil, water cannot enter to make them start growing. The seed coats are just too tough.

What the seed needs is some disturbance of the soil, such as digging by animals or plowing. This action scratches through the waterproof layer on the outside of the seed coat, allowing water in.

When land is newly plowed, a large crop of weeds often grows because of various seeds that have been lying in the soil for years.

Below: A Hakea bush carries thick, fireproof seed pods.

Fire can completely burn the Hakea leaves but only char the pods.

Left: A fire sweeps through dry bush in Western Australia. Some kinds of seeds cannot germinate until fire has burned the pods that contain them.

Other kinds of seeds will not grow until they have been chilled for several weeks. These seeds can be in warm, damp conditions outside for many months without germinating. If they are put in a refrigerator for a few weeks, however, and then planted outside, they start to grow. Refrigeration is like winter to the seeds. Because they had been through a "cold spell" and were then taken outside to warmer conditions, the seeds were tricked into "thinking" it was spring. Spring is the right time for seeds to be growing!

During cold and drought, seeds will not germinate. However, lupine seeds melted out of 10,000-year-old frozen **peat** from the Canadian Arctic will sometimes grow into new lupines.

Above: Elegant lupines grow in the mountains of North America. Their seeds can live for a long time, frozen in the ground.

A day or so after being charred, the Hakea pod splits...

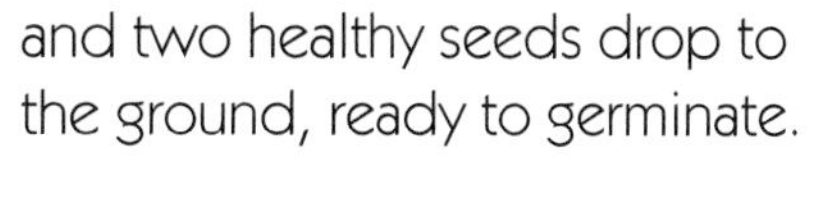

and two healthy seeds drop to the ground, ready to germinate.

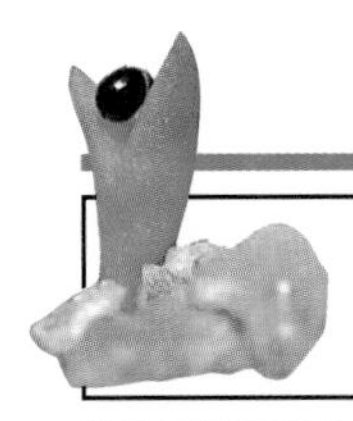

Can Seeds See?

Top: The black seed coat of a cactus seed wedges into the plant as the seedling grows.

Seeds do not have eyes like animals do, but there is no doubt that some seeds are able to detect light. What is even more remarkable is that seeds can distinguish between different colors of light.

The seeds of a variety of lettuce called Grand Rapids will not germinate in the dark, even if they are kept damp and warm. However, if pale red light is shone onto the damp seeds for just five minutes, they will germinate. It is as if the pale red light operates a switch that starts the process of germination.

Amazingly, the switch can be turned off again by a five-minute burst of deep red light applied immediately after the pale red burst.

Below: These lettuce seeds kept in the dark will not germinate — even if they are damp and warm.

A short burst of pale red light is all that is needed to cause some kinds of lettuce seeds to grow.

Left: Heather seeds wait until the ground has been disturbed and they can "see" light before they germinate.

Below: Heather produces small seeds with tiny food stores. If the seeds are buried deeply, the shoots will not have enough energy to burst out of the ground.

The reason some seeds are sensitive to light is that they need to avoid germinating when they are buried in the ground. A small seed does not have enough stored food to send its shoot up to the surface from deep underground. The shoot dies before it gets there. The seed must wait until the ground is disturbed, which brings it to the surface, before it can safely germinate. Small seeds of heather may lie in the ground for as long as eighty years, waiting to see the light. Only when the ground is disturbed and the seeds are brought to the surface, do they start to grow.

Traveling Seeds

Top: Each seed of a Norway maple is attached to a strong wing. The seeds spin like propellers as they fall from the tree.

Seeds need to travel in order to find new ground to grow in. A tree seed that falls to the ground beneath its parent tree does not have much of a chance to grow because it will always be shaded by the larger tree above. A seed that travels to open ground has a better chance of growing.

Seeds find many different ways to travel. Some are hitchhikers. They attach themselves to the fur of animals and then drop off at a new location. Many of these seed hitchhikers are **burrs** with sharp hooks that become entangled in fur.

Some grass seeds have a different method of hitching onto fur. Instead of hooks, each grass seed has an **awn** that contains thousands of tiny backward-pointing bristles. The bristles allow the seed to move forward, but not backward, through an animal's fur.

Below: A damp storksbill seed, with its straight awn, drops from the plant.

The next day in the hot, dry air, the awn starts to bend.

It curls around into a loop.

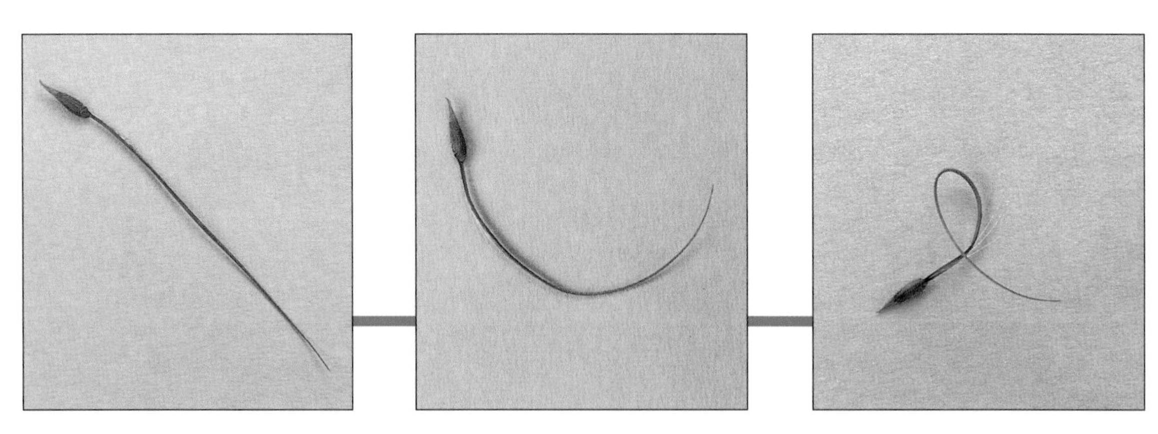

Left: Hooked bristles cover the seeds of plants called cleavers.

Below: The seeds of lesser burdock carry sharp hooks that fasten onto fur or wool.

As a furry animal wanders through tall grasses, seeds work their way into its coat. The seeds drop off later on during the animal's journey.

The seeds of storksbill and its relatives use their own power to "corkscrew" their way across the ground, and even into it. When the seeds are damp, the awns are straight. When the seeds become dry, however, the awns quickly twist into tight corkscrews. Moist nights and hot, dry days cause storksbill seeds to twist and untwist. Using corkscrew power, they creep away from their parent plant and find a fresh, new home.

As the awn twists, the seed moves across the ground.

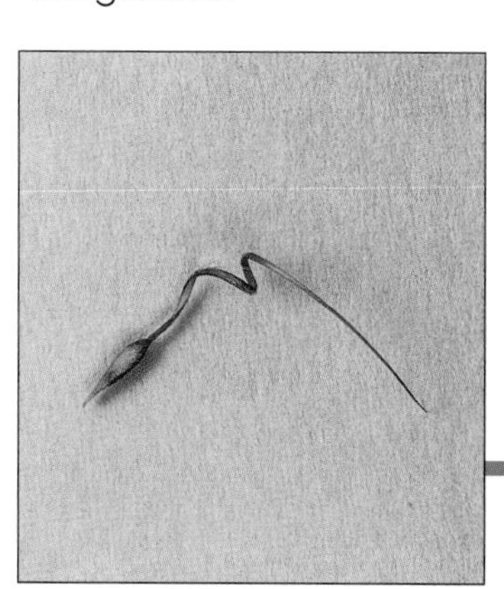

Another twist of the corkscrew, and the seed moves again.

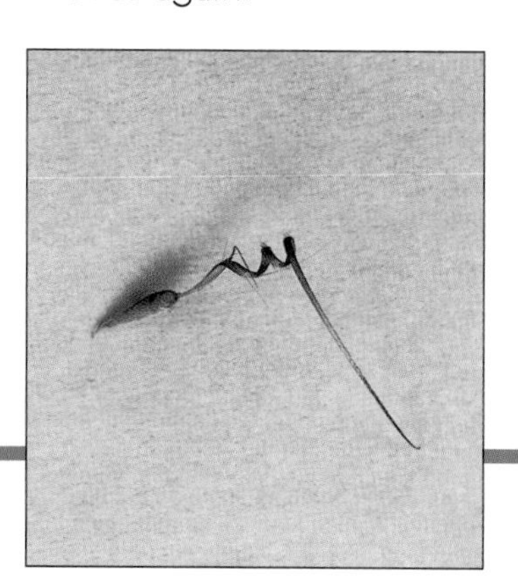

After five twists, the seed has moved 0.4 inch (1 centimeter).

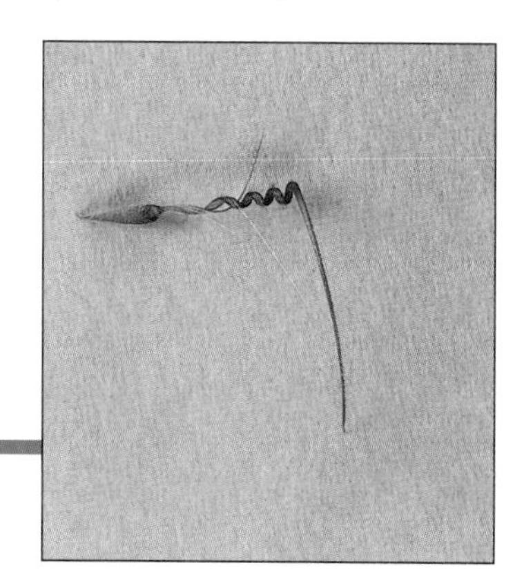

Above: The seed of the alsomitra vine is found in a thin, papery wing. The seed's weight causes the wing to glide gracefully to the ground.

Some seeds do not need to hitch a ride on an animal. They travel on the wind or even on water. The tiny seeds of willow trees have tufts of fine threads attached to them. When the wind blows, the tufts are caught up in it. The wind carries the seeds long distances. Cotton seeds have similar threads on them. The threads are so strong that cotton cloth is made from them.

Thistle seeds have parachutes made of stiff ribs with rows of fine hairs attached. Dandelion seeds hang beneath beautifully constructed parachutes. The bigger and stronger the parachute, the more weight it can carry. Elaborate parachutes carry big seeds that stand a good chance of growing into new plants.

Right: The parachutes of thistledown are attached directly to the seeds.

There is a limit to the size of seed that can be carried by a parachute. Some trees with large seeds have **evolved** a way of keeping the seeds airborne. Each seed has a wing, or in some species, two wings, that cause the entire seed to spin as it falls. Large seeds on spinning propellers can be carried several hundred feet (meters) in a strong wind. Wings on seeds do not always make them spin. The paper-thin wings of alsomitra seeds allow the seeds to glide over 330 feet (100 meters) through the still air of the tropical rain forests of Asia.

Above: The parachutes of dandelion seeds form a ball-shape on each flower stem. A field of dandelions in seed looks like a field of fluffy balls. When the wind blows, each seed flies separately.

Right: Each of these long goatsbeard seeds has a thin stalk with a parachute on the end.

Seedy Fruits

Top: Each yew tree seed is surrounded by a red berry that birds enjoy eating.

Hitchhikers do not expect to pay for their ride. Burrs give nothing to the animals that carry them, but there are many plants that do reward the animals that carry their seeds. The reward is a juicy fruit or berry.

When a bird eats a berry, it usually swallows the seeds that are in it. The seeds are later regurgitated or passed out in the bird's droppings, far from the plant that produced the berry. The seeds have hitched a ride, and the bird has received a reward. The seeds in berries must have a strong seed coat to avoid being digested in the bird's stomach. They also must be small enough to be swallowed with the berry.

Right: The red fruits of quondong are especially attractive to emus. The seeds are ready to germinate after they have passed through an emu's body.

Left: This jackal dropping on the sandy shore of southwestern Africa contains many desert melon seeds. After a rainfall, the seeds could germinate.

Above: The black seeds of coastal wattle are surrounded by a red, edible stalk.

Large seeds stand a better chance of growing into new plants than small seeds. However, large seeds from oak trees and other nut trees may run a greater risk of being eaten and fully digested by animals. Seeds that are fully digested do not return to the soil for germination.

However, these trees are still successful. They produce many more seeds in autumn than can be eaten by animals at one time. The animals bury the extra seeds so they can eat them later. Although some animals have very good memories, every buried seed is not retrieved by them. In spring, the forgotten seeds sprout from their comfortable resting places in the soil.

Below: An ant collects a coastal wattle seed. It will feed the red stalk to its **larvae**, leaving the seed to germinate.

Spring-loaded Pods

Top: This sweet pea pod contains a row of green, unripe seeds.

Above: A ripe pod of Himalayan balsam explodes, sending the seeds showering in all directions.

Some seeds form in pods. An example of this is the pea plant. When pea pods are ripe, they split open, and the peas (seeds) fall out.

Gorse bushes and broom bushes belong to the same family as peas, and they have similar pods. The pods dry in the summer Sun until, finally, they split into two halves.

The splitting happens with a loud crack, as the two halves of the pod twist apart. After each crack, a patter of seeds rains down. The cracking pods throw the small seeds into the air. Some of the seeds land more than 6 feet (2 m) away from the bush.

Right: The flat pods of honesty contain flat seeds that scatter with the wind.

Gorse and broom bushes can throw seeds because the walls of their pods act like twisted springs. When the pods split, the springs are released, throwing the seeds.

Other plants throw their seeds even farther. Balsam seeds are held tightly in their pods, each seed sitting on its own spring. As the pod dries, it becomes weaker and the springs become stronger until the pod can hold only the force of the springs. A ripe balsam pod needs only the slightest touch to explode.

Above: Green, unripe broom pods turn black when they are ripe. Then, they burst, throwing their seeds high into the air.

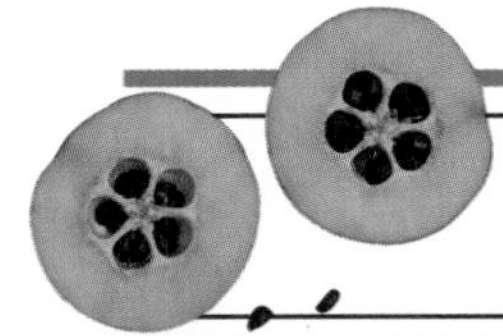

Seeds as Food

Top: The brown seeds of Japonica form in five pockets within a hard, bitter fruit.

The little point on the end of a grain of wheat is the embryo. The rest of the grain is endosperm, which is mostly starch. Starch provides food for the growing embryo. It is also food for birds and other animals. Many species of birds eat only seeds. Mice and rats also search out seeds that provide a healthy diet for them.

Surprisingly, people eat seeds more than any other food. In fact, humans mainly eat grass seeds — wheat and rice are two types of grass!

Many seeds contain oil. Most of the cooking oils people use are extracted from the seeds of plants — for instance, sunflowers and olives. Oil and starch are important foods for animals as well as humans.

Above: A goldfinch uses its sharply pointed beak to take the seeds out of teasel heads.

Right: A spotted grass mouse eats an acacia seed.

Left: Even a macaw with its massively strong beak has a difficult time cracking the hard shell of a Brazil nut.

Plants, of course, do not want their seeds to be eaten. Some seeds, or nuts, are encased in hard shells to make them difficult to eat. The shells of Brazil and macadamia nuts are so tough that animals have to work very hard for a reward. Some animals just give up and drop these nuts. The nuts can then grow into new trees.

Another way in which plants make their seeds less attractive is to give them a bad taste. If you have ever bitten into an orange or apple pip, or seed, you know how bitter it is. Perhaps you have even spit the pip out on the ground. In this way, you actually planted a seed!

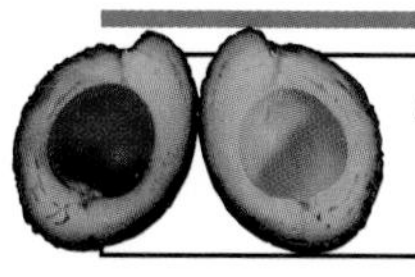

The Numbers Game

Top: An avocado tree puts a lot of energy into growing each big seed.

Plants have a limited amount of energy to spare for producing seeds. So which factors do you think determine whether a plant produces a few big seeds or many little ones? If the plant is a big tree, such as an oak or chestnut, it may produce about a thousand large seeds. When all the energy in a big tree goes into producing little seeds, however, it produces millions of seeds. Willow trees, for example, produce millions of tiny seeds.

Some plants use large amounts of energy to produce just a few seeds. The palm tree called coco-de-mer produces the largest seeds of all. Its enormous seeds take up to ten years to grow. Each seed and its husk weighs nearly 55 pounds (25 kilograms). The coconut palm produces a similar large seed, encased in a spongy husk that can float. Each coconut is about 12 inches (30 centimeters) long. Coconuts often float away at sea until they land on a beach and germinate.

Orchids produce the smallest seeds. Orchid pods contain thousands of seeds so tiny that they look — and blow around — like dust. Orchid seeds have no food store. They need **fungi** for food when they germinate. Orchids have to produce vast numbers of seeds because the chance of a seed finding the right fungus is very small.

Above: Sweet chestnut seeds are so large that even a big tree can produce only about a thousand of them.

Opposite: Coconut palms produce seeds inside oval-shaped, fibrous outer husks and hard inner shells.

Below: Each orchid flower produces thousands of tiny seeds.

Moving Without Seeds

Top: Bracken shoots up from an underground stem.

Some plants travel by means other than their seeds. Bramble bushes, which are members of the rose family, produce long, thorny stems that creep over the ground at up to 2 inches (5 cm) a day during summer. When autumn comes, these stems sprout roots at their tips, and form new plants. Brambles march over the ground to quickly cover large areas.

Some plants, such as bracken from the fern family, may have underground stems that send up shoots at intervals. Bracken marches invisibly onto new ground until the shoots appear. Entire hillsides may become covered with the shoots of just one bracken plant.

Above: Brambles spread quickly by means of long stems that reach out and sprout roots. Even a broken-off leaf of a bramble will sprout roots.

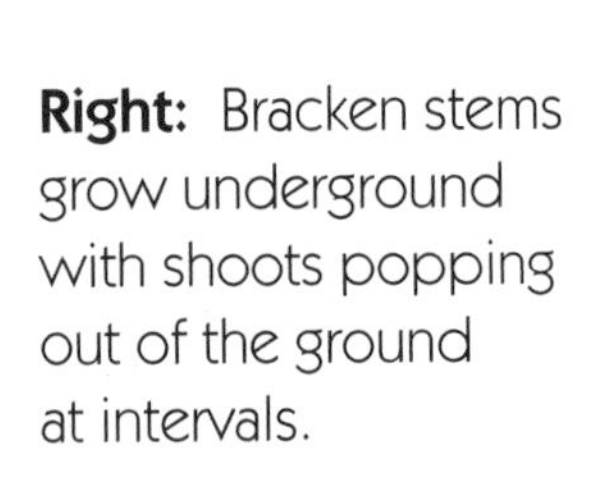

Right: Bracken stems grow underground with shoots popping out of the ground at intervals.

Left: Dead tumbleweeds roll along in the wind, dropping seeds in various places.

In addition, an entire plant or part of one can uproot and travel. The stems of tumbleweed, for example, curl inward as the plant dies, forming a rounded mass that tumbles along in the wind. The tumbleweed plant drops its seeds as it travels. As winter approaches, the shoots of bladderwort form balls and break off the plant. The green plant balls drift around in the slow streams where the plant once grew. When spring comes, they grow into new plants.

Above: The shoots of the water plant, lesser bladderwort, form balls that break off in winter. In spring, the balls unroll, as one has done here, and start to grow.

There are many children's stories about magical seeds. In "Jack and the Beanstalk," a boy named Jack must sell his cow for gold to support his family. Instead of gold, he comes home with some magic beans that grow into an incredibly tall plant that reaches another world.

You do not need to read fairy tales to see how magical seeds are. A small, smooth, shiny seed can sprout into a beautiful tree with scented flowers. That is real magic!

Activities:

Sensitive Seeds

Right: Press the seeds against the glass on the inside of the jar. Fill the center of the jar with sand.

Seeds need water before they can begin to grow. Big seeds generally take longer to grow than small seeds. Some of the tiniest seeds start growing within just a few hours after watering.

A small, white point coming out of a seed is the first sign of germination. This is the tip of the root. Roots grow downward. Later, a shoot will appear and grow upward.

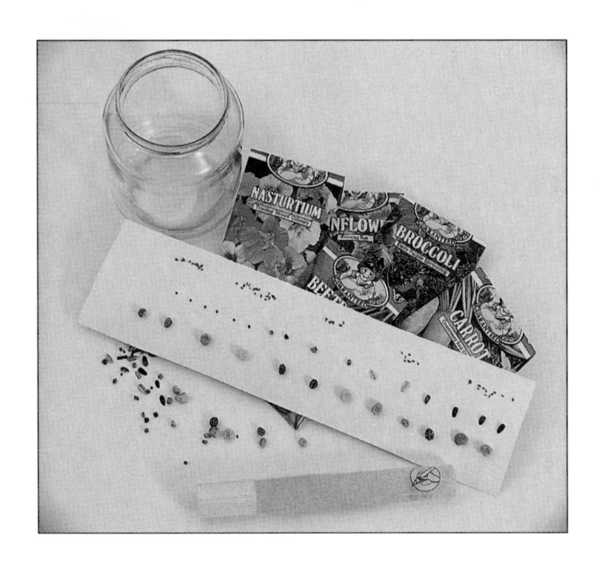

Observe the process by growing seeds in a jar. You will need a large glass jar with straight sides, blotting paper, scissors, glue, clean sand (silver sand from a pet store), and various kinds of seeds, large and small *(see above)*. Cut a strip of blotting paper to snugly fit the walls inside the jar.

With small blobs of glue, stick a variety of seeds to one side of the paper. You can arrange the seeds in a pattern or dot them here and there at random. Allow enough space between the seeds so they will have plenty of room to grow.

When the glue has set, gently roll the paper up, with the seeds on the outside. Carefully place the paper into the jar. Make sure the paper expands in the jar so that the seeds are pressed against the glass. Pour dry sand into the jar to hold the blotting paper and seeds in place.

Slowly pour water into your seed garden until all the sand is damp, and a little water is visible at the bottom of the jar. Put the jar in the sunlight. Wait and watch.

The first thing you may notice is that the glass on the inside of the jar will start to steam up.

Look carefully at the pattern of steam on the glass. You may find that there is a circle of clear glass around each of the bigger seeds. This is because the seeds are grabbing water and soaking it up.

As the seeds soak up water, they swell until the tips of their roots appear. Small seeds germinate quickly, but they do not grow for very long. This is because they have small food stores. Bigger seeds may take longer to germinate but grow for a long time, using their large food stores. Keep the jar in sunlight. Turn it each day.

Little Creeps

Animals will sometimes carry grass seeds, but grass seeds do not have hooks that catch animals' fur or wool.

Instead, the seeds and their awns are covered in fine bristles, all pointing the same way. The bristles cause the seeds to creep into fur or wool. People sometimes carry grass seeds, too, in their socks or other pieces of clothing after walking through a grassy area, such as a hayfield.

To understand how seeds attach in this way, get some barley, whiskered wheat, or rye seeds.

Separate a seed from the seed head and rub it gently, lengthways, between your finger and thumb *(below, left)*.

Never put a grass seed in your mouth. It could creep down your throat, causing you to choke. Grass seeds also sometimes creep into dogs' or cats' ears, causing a lot of trouble for them.

As you rub the seed, it will creep out of your grasp. In the same way, grass seeds use their bristles to creep into the fur or woolly coats of animals. The seeds may creep right through the fur or wool — dropping off later, after the animal has traveled to another area.

Below: The spiked seeds of doublegee travel by piercing animals' feet. Here, many seeds have stuck into the sole of a boot.

Glossary

awn: a stiff bristle on seeds or other parts of plants.

burr: a seed with small hooks that clings to fur, wool, and clothing.

cell: a microscopic building block of plant and animal bodies.

Centigrade: a temperature scale that is divided into one hundred degrees. The freezing point of water is at 0°, and the boiling point of water is at 100°.

cotyledon: the first leaf or one of the first pair or whorl of leaves developed by the embryo of a seed plant.

dicotyledon: a group of plants, including peas, beans, and most flowering plants, with seedlings that always have two cotyledons.

embryo: a plant or animal in the early stages of development.

endosperm: the part of most seeds where food is stored.

evolved: changed and improved gradually over time.

Fahrenheit: a temperature scale with the freezing point of water at 32° and the boiling point of water at 212°.

food store: the part of a seed that contains food for the growing embryo. The embryo is joined to the food store.

fungi: a major division of the plant kingdom. Fungi are considered parasitic lower plants and lack chlorophyll. Mushrooms, mildew, molds, and rust are fungi. *Fungus* is the singular.

germinate: to start to grow. A seed germinates and grows into a new plant. The smaller the seed, the faster it germinates.

larvae: young stages in the growth of insects and some other animals.

micropyle: a tiny hole in the seed coat through which water can enter a seed.

minerals: simple chemicals or compounds found in the soil.

monocotyledon: a group of plants, including all grasses and lilies, with seedlings that always have only one cotyledon.

ova: the female cells from which seeds (or animals) develop. *Ovum* is the singular.

oxygen: a gas, essential for life, that forms one-fifth of the air.

peat: material formed from the compressed stems and leaves of plants that have been dead for a long time.

pod: a container for seeds.

pollen: male cells, in the form of fine grains, that are produced by flowers.

protein: a substance containing nitrogen.

root: the normally underground part of a plant that absorbs water and minerals.

seed coat: the tough coating on the outside of a seed.

shoot: a young, rapidly growing part of a plant that reaches upward.

starch: a carbohydrate that occurs in nature, particularly in plants.

Plants and Animals

The common names of plants and animals vary from language to language. But plants and animals also have scientific names, based on Greek or Latin words, that are the same the world over. Each plant and animal has two scientific names. The first name is called the genus. It starts with a capital letter. The second name is the species name. It starts with a small letter.

beech *(Fagus sylvatica)* — Europe 9, 10

bracken *(Pteridium aquifolium)* — worldwide 26

Brazil nut *(Bertholletia excelsa)* — South America 23

broom *(Cytisus scoparius)* — Europe 21

cleavers *(Galium aparine)* — Europe 15

dandelion *(Taraxacum officinale)* — Europe, introduced elsewhere cover, 17

elegant lupine *(Lupinus lepidus)* — North America 11

giant sequoia *(Sequoiadendron giganteum)* — western North America 4, 5

goatsbeard *(Tragopogon pratensis)* — Europe 17

Hakea *(Hakea cristata)* — Australia 10-11

heather *(Calluna vulgaris)* — Europe 13

Himalayan balsam *(Impatiens glandulifera)* — Asia, introduced elsewhere 20, 21

honesty *(Lunaria annua)* — Europe 20

lesser bladderwort *(Utricularia minor)* — Europe 27

lesser burdock *(Arctium minus)* — Europe 15

lettuce *(Lactuca sativa)* — cultivated worldwide 12

macaw *(Ara araruana)* — South America 23

Norway maple *(Acer platanoides)* — Europe 14

peanut *(Arachis hypogaea)* — South America, cultivated elsewhere 5

quondong *(Santalum acuminatum)* — Australia 18

scarlet runner bean *(Phaseolus coccineus)* — South America, cultivated elsewhere 8

spotted grass mouse *(Lemniscomys striatus)* — Africa 22

storksbill *(Erodium cicutarium)* — Europe, introduced elsewhere 14-15

Books to Read

All About Seeds. M. Berger (Scholastic)

Bloodthirsty Plants (series). Victor Gentle (Gareth Stevens)

Flowers. Joy Richardson (Franklin Watts)

How a Seed Grows. Helene J. Jordan (HarperCollins)

How Seeds Travel. Cynthia Overbeck (Lerner Group)

The Magic School Bus Plants Seeds: A Book About How Living Things Grow. Patricia Relf (Scholastic)

The Nature and Science of Flowers. Exploring the Science of Nature (series). Jane Burton and Kim Taylor (Gareth Stevens)

Seeds to Plants. Jeffrey Bates (Glouscester)

Videos and Web Sites

Videos

A Flowering Plant from Seed to Seed. (International Film Bureau)
All About Seeds. (Film Ideas, Inc.)
How Plants Grow. (United Learning)
How Seeds Get Here ... and There. (MBG Videos)
What's Inside a Seed? (Coronet, The Multimedia Co.)

Web Sites

www.dole5aday.com/about/citrus.oranges/html
www.arborday.net/kids/kid_links.htm
www.icangarden.com/kidz.htm
stellar.arc.nasa.gov/stellar/Activities/hydro/ShuttleMirSeedGerm/SeedGerm.html
www.lycos.com/wguide/network/net_969333.html

Some web sites stay current longer than others. For further web sites, use your search engines to locate the following topics: *awns, cotyledons, germination, plants, pods, seeds,* and *trees.*

Index